P9-BXX-300

THE BED OF PROCRUSTES

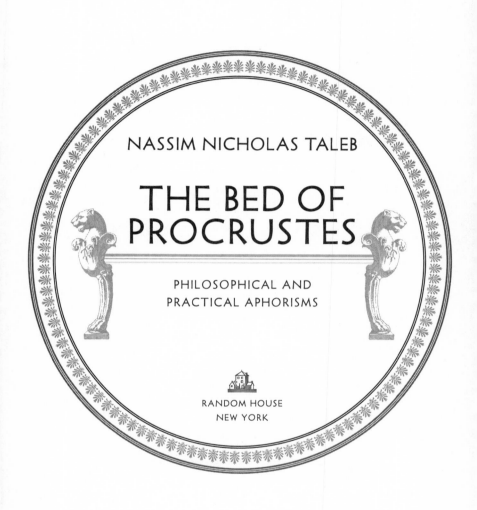

NASSIM NICHOLAS TALEB

THE BED OF PROCRUSTES

PHILOSOPHICAL AND
PRACTICAL APHORISMS

RANDOM HOUSE
NEW YORK

Copyright © 2010 by Nassim Nicholas Taleb

All rights reserved.

Published in the United States by Random House, an imprint of
The Random House Publishing Group, a division of Random
House, Inc., New York.

RANDOM HOUSE and colophon are registered trademarks of
Random House, Inc.

Library of Congress Cataloging-in-Publication Data
Taleb, Nassim.
The bed of Procrustes: philosophical and practical aphorisms /
by Nassim Nicholas Taleb.
p. cm.
ISBN 978-1-4000-6997-2
eBook ISBN 978-0-679-64368-5
1. Aphorisms and apothegms.   2. Human behavior—
Quotations, maxims, etc.   I. Title.
PN6271.T35 2011
818'.602—dc22
2010036866

Printed in the United States of America on acid-free paper

www.atrandom.com

2 4 6 8 9 7 5 3 1

FIRST EDITION

Book design by Simon M. Sullivan

To Alexander N. Taleb

CONTENTS

CONTENTS

PROCRUSTES

Procrustes, in Greek mythology, was the cruel owner of a small estate in Corydalus in Attica, on the way between Athens and Eleusis, where the mystery rites were performed. Procrustes had a peculiar sense of hospitality: he abducted travelers, provided them with a generous dinner, then invited them to spend the night in a rather special bed. He wanted the bed to fit the traveler to perfection. Those who were too tall had their legs chopped off with a sharp hatchet; those who were too short were stretched (his name was said to be Damastes, or Polyphemon, but he was nicknamed Procrustes, which meant "the stretcher").

In the purest of poetic justice, Procrustes was hoisted by his own petard. One of the travelers happened to be the fearless Theseus, who slayed the Minotaur later in his heroic career. After the customary dinner, Theseus made Procrustes lie in his own bed. Then, to make him fit in it to the customary perfection, he decapitated him. Theseus thus followed Hercules's method of paying back in kind.

In more sinister versions (such as the one in Pseudo-Apollodorus's *Bibliotheca*), Procrustes owned two beds, one small, one large; he made short victims lie in the large bed, and the tall victims in the short one.

Every aphorism here is about a Procrustean bed of sorts—we humans, facing limits of knowledge, and things we do not observe, the unseen and the unknown, resolve the tension by squeezing life and the world into crisp commoditized ideas, reductive categories, specific vocabularies, and prepackaged narratives, which, on the occasion, has explosive consequences. Further, we seem unaware of this backward fitting, much like tailors who take great pride in delivering the perfectly fitting suit—but do so by surgically altering the limbs of their customers. For instance, few realize that we are changing the brains of schoolchildren through medication in order to make them adjust to the curriculum, rather than the reverse.

Since aphorisms lose their charm whenever explained, I only hint for now at the central theme of this book—I relegate further discussions to the postface. These are standalone compressed thoughts revolving around my main idea of *how we deal, and should deal, with what we don't know,* matters more deeply discussed in my books *The Black Swan* and *Fooled by Randomness.**

---

* My use of the metaphor of the Procrustes bed isn't just about putting something in the wrong box; it's mostly that inverse operation of changing the wrong variable, here the person rather than the bed. Note that every failure of what we call "wisdom" (coupled with technical proficiency) can be reduced to a Procrustean bed situation.

THE BED OF PROCRUSTES

PRELUDES

The person you are the most afraid to contradict is yourself.

—

An idea starts to be interesting when you get scared of taking it to its logical conclusion.

—

Pharmaceutical companies are better at inventing diseases that match existing drugs, rather than inventing drugs to match existing diseases.

To understand the liberating effect of asceticism, consider that losing all your fortune is much less painful than losing only half of it.

—

To bankrupt a fool, give him information.

—

Academia is to knowledge what prostitution is to love; close enough on the surface but, to the nonsucker, not exactly the same thing.*

—

In science you need to understand the world; in business you need others to misunderstand it.

—

I suspect that they put Socrates to death because there is something terribly unattractive, alienating, and nonhuman in thinking with too much clarity.

---

* I need a qualifier here. There are exceptions, but there are also many known cases in which a prostitute falls in love with a client.

Education makes the wise slightly wiser, but it makes the fool vastly more dangerous.

—

The test of originality for an idea is not the absence of one single predecessor but the presence of multiple but incompatible ones.

—

Modernity's double punishment is to make us both age prematurely and live longer.

—

An erudite is someone who displays less than he knows; a journalist or consultant, the opposite.

—

Your brain is most intelligent when you don't instruct it on what to do—something people who take showers discover on occasion.

If your anger decreases with time, you did injustice; if it increases, you suffered injustice.

—

I wonder if those who advocate generosity for its rewards notice the inconsistency, or if what they call generosity is an attractive investment strategy.*

—

Those who think religion is about "belief" don't understand religion, and don't understand belief.

—

Work destroys your soul by stealthily invading your brain during the hours not officially spent working; be selective about professions.

---

* A generous act is precisely what should aim at no reward, neither financial nor social nor emotional; deontic (unconditional observance of duties), not utilitarian (aiming at some collective—or even individual—gains in welfare). There is nothing wrong with "generous" acts that elicit a "warm glow" or promise salvation to the giver; these are not to be linguistically conflated with deontic actions, those emanating from pure sense of duty.

In nature we never repeat the same motion; in captivity (office, gym, commute, sports), life is just repetitive-stress injury. No randomness.

—

Using, as an excuse, others' failure of common sense is in itself a failure of common sense.

—

Compliance with the straitjacket of narrow (Aristotelian) logic and avoidance of fatal inconsistencies are not the same thing.

—

Economics cannot digest the idea that the collective (and the aggregate) are disproportionately less predictable than individuals.

—

Don't talk about "progress" in terms of longevity, safety, or comfort before comparing zoo animals to those in the wilderness.

If you know, in the morning, what your day looks like with any precision, you are a little bit dead—the more precision, the more dead you are.

—

There is no intermediate state between ice and water but there is one between life and death: employment.

—

You have a calibrated life when most of what you fear has the titillating prospect of adventure.

—

Procrastination is the soul rebelling against entrapment.

—

Nobody wants to be perfectly transparent; not to others, certainly not to himself.

COUNTER
NARRATIVES

The best revenge on a liar is to convince him that you believe what he said.

—

When we want to do something while unconsciously certain to fail, we seek advice so we can blame someone else for the failure.

—

It is harder to say *no* when you really mean it than when you don't.

Never say *no* twice if you mean it.

—

Your reputation is harmed the most by what you say to defend it.

—

The only objective definition of aging is when a person starts to talk about aging.

—

They will envy you for your success, for your wealth, for your intelligence, for your looks, for your status— but rarely for your wisdom.

—

Most of what they call humility is successfully disguised arrogance.

If you want people to read a book, tell them it is overrated.

—

You never win an argument until they attack your person.

—

Nothing is more permanent than "temporary" arrangements, deficits, truces, and relationships; and nothing is more temporary than "permanent" ones.

—

The most painful moments are not those we spend with uninteresting people; rather, they are those spent with uninteresting people trying hard to be interesting.

—

Hatred is love with a typo somewhere in the computer code, correctable but very hard to find.

I wonder whether a bitter enemy would be jealous if he discovered that I hated someone else.

—

The characteristic feature of the loser is to bemoan, in general terms, mankind's flaws, biases, contradictions, and irrationality—without exploiting them for fun and profit.

—

The test of whether you really liked a book is if you reread it (and how many times); the test of whether you really liked someone's company is if you are ready to meet him again and again—the rest is spin, or that variety of sentiment now called self-esteem.

—

We ask "why is he rich (or poor)?" not "why isn't he richer (or poorer)?"; "why is the crisis so deep?" not "why isn't it deeper?"

Hatred is much harder to fake than love. You hear of fake love; never of fake hate.

—

The opposite of manliness isn't cowardice; it's technology.

—

Usually, what we call a "good listener" is someone with skillfully polished indifference.

—

It is the appearance of inconsistency, and not its absence, that makes people attractive.

—

You remember emails you sent that were not answered better than emails that you did not answer.

People reserve standard compliments for those who do not threaten their pride; the others they often praise by calling "arrogant."

—

Since Cato the Elder, a certain type of maturity has shown up when one starts blaming the new generation for "shallowness" and praising the previous one for its "values."

—

It is as difficult to avoid bugging others with advice on how to exercise and other health matters as it is to stick to an exercise schedule.

—

By praising someone for his lack of defects you are also implying his lack of virtues.

—

When she shouts that what you did was unforgivable, she has already started to forgive you.

Being unimaginative is only a problem when you are easily bored.

—

We call narcissistic those individuals who behave as if they were the central residents of the world; those who do exactly the same in a set of two we call lovers or, better, "blessed by love."

—

Friendship that ends was never one; there was at least one sucker in it.

—

Most people fear being without audiovisual stimulation because they are too repetitive when they think and imagine things on their own.

—

Unrequited hate is vastly more diminishing for the self than unrequited love. You can't react by reciprocating.

For the compassionate, sorrow is more easily displaced by another sorrow than by joy.

—

Wisdom in the young is as unattractive as frivolity in the elderly.

—

Some people are only funny when they try to be serious.

—

It is difficult to stop the impulse to reveal secrets in conversation, as if information had the desire to live and the power to multiply.

MATTERS
ONTOLOGICAL

It is a very recent disease to mistake the unobserved for the nonexistent; but some are plagued with the worse disease of mistaking the unobserved for the unobservable.

—

Asking science to explain life and vital matters is equivalent to asking a grammarian to explain poetry.

—

You exist if and only if you are free to do things without a visible objective, with no justification and, above all, outside the dictatorship of someone else's narrative.

THE SACRED
AND
THE PROFANE

You cannot express the holy in terms made for the profane, but you can discuss the profane in terms made for the holy.

—

Atheism (materialism) means treating the dead as if they were unborn. I won't. By accepting the sacred, you reinvent religion.

If you can't spontaneously detect (without analyzing) the difference between sacred and profane, you'll never know what religion means. You will also never figure out what we commonly call art. You will never understand anything.

—

People used to wear ordinary clothes weekdays and formal attire on Sunday. Today it is the exact reverse.

—

To mark a separation between holy and profane, I take a ritual bath after any contact, or correspondence (even emails), with consultants, economists, Harvard Business School professors, journalists, and those in similarly depraved pursuits; I then feel and act purified from the profane until the next episode.

The book is the only medium left that hasn't been corrupted by the profane: everything else on your eyelids manipulates you with an ad.*

—

You can replace lies with truth; but myth is only displaced with a narrative.

—

The sacred is all about unconditionals; the profane is all about conditionals.†

—

The source of the tragic in history is in mistaking someone else's unconditional for conditional—and the reverse.

---

* A comment here. After a long diet from the media, I came to realize that there is nothing that's not (clumsily) trying to sell you something. I only trust my library. There is nothing wrong with the ownership of the physical book as a manifestation of human weakness, desire to show off, peacock tail–style signaling of superiority, it's the commercial agenda outside the book that corrupts.
† For instance, many people said to be unbribable are just too expensive.

Restaurants get you in with food to sell you liquor; religions get you in with belief to sell you rules (e.g., avoid debt). People can understand the notion of God, not unexplained rules, interdicts, and categorical heuristics.

—

One categorical: it is easier to fast than diet. You cannot be "slightly" kosher or halal by only eating a small portion of ham.

—

To be completely cured of newspapers, spend a year reading the previous week's newspapers.

CHANCE, SUCCESS, HAPPINESS, AND STOICISM

Success is becoming in middle adulthood what you dreamed to be in late childhood. The rest comes from loss of control.

—

The opposite of success isn't failure; it is name-dropping.

—

Modernity needs to understand that being rich and becoming rich are not mathematically, personally, socially, and ethically the same thing.

You don't become completely free by just avoiding to be a slave; you also need to avoid becoming a master.*

–

Fortune punishes the greedy by making him poor and the very greedy by making him rich.

–

Quite revealing of human preferences that more suicides come from shame or loss of financial and social status than medical diagnoses.

–

"Wealthy" is meaningless and has no robust absolute measure; use intead the subtractive measure "unwealth," that is, the difference, at any point in time, between what you have and what you would like to have.

* Versions of this point have been repeated and rediscovered throughout history—the last convincing one by Montaigne.

Older people are most beautiful when they have what is lacking in the young: poise, erudition, wisdom, phronesis, and this post-heroic absence of agitation.

—

I went to a happiness conference; researchers looked very unhappy.

—

What fools call "wasting time" is most often the best investment.

—

Decline starts with the replacement of dreams with memories and ends with the replacement of memories with other memories.

—

You want to avoid being disliked without being envied or admired.

Read nothing from the past one hundred years; eat no fruits from the past one thousand years; drink nothing from the past four thousand years (just wine and water); but talk to no ordinary man over forty. A man without a heroic bent starts dying at the age of thirty.

Some pursuits are much duller from the inside. Even piracy, they say.

Karl Marx, a visionary, figured out that you can control a slave much better by convincing him he is an employee.

Catholic countries had more serial monogamy than today, but without the need for divorce—life expectancy was short; marriage duration was much, much shorter.

The fastest way to become rich is to socialize with the poor; the fastest way to become poor is to socialize with the rich.

—

You will be civilized on the day you can spend a long period doing nothing, learning nothing, and improving nothing, without feeling the slightest amount of guilt.

—

Someone who says "I am busy" is either declaring incompetence (and lack of control of his life) or trying to get rid of you.

—

The difference between slaves in Roman and Ottoman days and today's employees is that slaves did not need to flatter their boss.

You are rich if and only if money you refuse tastes better than money you accept.

—

For most, success is the harmful passage from the camp of the hating to the camp of the hated.

—

To see if you like where you are, without the chains of dependence, check if you are as happy returning as you were leaving.

—

The difference between love and happiness is that those who talk about love tend to be in love, but those who talk about happiness tend to be not happy.

—

Modernity: we created youth without heroism, age without wisdom, and life without grandeur.

You can tell how uninteresting a person is by asking him whom he finds interesting.

—

The Web is an unhealthy place for someone hungry for attention.

—

I wonder if anyone ever measured the time it takes, at a party, before a mildly successful stranger who went to Harvard makes others aware of it.

—

People focus on role models; it is more effective to find antimodels—people you don't want to resemble when you grow up.

—

It is a good practice to always apologize, except when you have done something wrong.

Preoccupation with efficacy is the main obstacle to a poetic, noble, elegant, robust, and heroic life.

—

Some, like most bankers, are so unfit for success that they look like dwarves dressed in giants' clothes.

—

Don't complain too loud about wrongs done you; you may give ideas to your less imaginative enemies.

—

Most feed their obsessions by trying to get rid of them.

—

It is as difficult to change someone's opinions as it is to change his tastes.

I have the fondest memories of time spent in places called ugly, the most boring ones of places called scenic.

—

Fitness is certainly the sign of strength, but outside of natural stimuli the drive to acquire fitness can signal some deep incurable weakness.

—

Charm is the ability to insult people without offending them; nerdiness the reverse.

—

Those who do not think that employment is systemic slavery are either blind or employed.

They are born, then put in a box; they go home to live in a box; they study by ticking boxes; they go to what is called "work" in a box, where they sit in their cubicle box; they drive to the grocery store in a box to buy food in a box; they go to the gym in a box to sit in a box; they talk about thinking "outside the box"; and when they die they are put in a box. All boxes, Euclidian, geometrically smooth boxes.

—

Another definition of modernity: conversations can be more and more completely reconstructed with clips from other conversations taking place at the same time on the planet.

—

The twentieth century was the bankruptcy of the social utopia; the twenty-first will be that of the technological one.

Efforts at building social, political, and medical utopias have caused nightmares; many cures and techniques came from martial efforts.

—

The Web's "connectedness" creates a peculiar form of informational and pseudosocial promiscuity, which makes one feel clean after Web rationing.

—

In most debates, people seem to be trying to convince one another; but all they can hope for is new arguments to convince themselves.

CHARMING AND
LESS CHARMING
SUCKER PROBLEMS

The most depressing aspect of the lives of the couples you watch surreptitiously arguing in restaurants is that they are almost always unaware of the true subject of argument.

—

It seems that it is the most unsuccessful people who give the most advice, particularly for writing and financial matters.

—

Rumors are only valuable when they are denied.

Over the long term, you are more likely to fool yourself than others.

—

There are two types of people: those who try to win and those who try to win arguments. They are never the same.

—

People usually apologize so they can do it again.

—

Mathematics is to knowledge what an artificial hand is to the real one; some amputate to replace.

—

Modernity inflicts a sucker narrative on activities; now we "walk for exercise," not "walk" with no justification; for hidden reasons.

Social media are severely antisocial, health foods are empirically unhealthy, knowledge workers are very ignorant, and social sciences aren't scientific at all.

—

For so many, instead of looking for "cause of death" when they expire, we should be looking for "cause of life" when they are still around.

—

It is those who use others who are the most upset when someone uses them.

—

If someone gives you more than one reason why he wants the job, don't hire him.

—

Failure of second-order thinking: he tells you a secret and somehow expects you to keep it, when he just gave you evidence that he can't keep it himself.

Social networks present information about what people like; more informative if, instead, they described what they don't like.

—

People are so prone to overcausation that you can make the reticent turn loquacious by dropping an occasional "why?" in the conversation.

—

I need to keep reminding myself that a truly independent thinker may look like an accountant.

THESEUS,
OR LIVING
THE PALEO LIFE

The three most harmful addictions are heroin, carbohydrates, and a monthly salary.

—

My only measure of success is how much time you have to kill.

—

I wonder if a lion (or a cannibal) would pay a high premium for free-range humans.

If you need to listen to music while walking, don't walk; and please don't listen to music.

—

Men destroy each other during war; themselves during peacetime.

—

Sports feminize men and masculinize women.

—

Technology can degrade (and endanger) every aspect of a sucker's life while convincing him that it is becoming more "efficient."

—

The difference between technology and slavery is that slaves are fully aware that they are not free.

You have a real life if and only if you do not compete
with anyone in any of your pursuits.

—

With terminal disease, nature lets you die with
abbreviated suffering; medicine lets you suffer with
prolonged dying.

—

We are satisfied with natural (or old) objects like
vistas or classical paintings but insatiable with
technologies, amplifying small improvements in
versions, obsessed about 2.0, caught in a mental
treadmill.

—

Only in recent history has "working hard" signaled
pride rather than shame for lack of talent, finesse, and,
mostly, *sprezzatura*.

Their idea of the sabbatical is to work six days and rest for one; my idea of the sabbatical is to work for (part of) a day and rest for six.

—

What they call "play" (gym, travel, sports) looks like work; the harder they try, the more captive they are.

—

Most modern efficiencies are deferred punishment.

—

We are hunters; we are only truly alive in those moments when we improvise; no schedule, just small surprises and stimuli from the environment.

—

For everything, use boredom in place of a clock, as a biological wristwatch, though under constraints of politeness.

Decomposition, for most, starts when they leave the free, social, and uncorrupted college life for the solitary confinement of professions and nuclear families.

—

For a classicist, a competitive athlete is painful to look at; trying hard to become an animal rather than a man, he will never be as fast as a cheetah or as strong as an ox.

—

Skills that transfer: street fights, off-path hiking, seduction, broad erudition. Skills that don't: school, games, sports, laboratory—what's reduced and organized.

—

You exist in full if and only if your conversation (or writings) cannot be easily reconstructed with clips from other conversations.

—

The English have random Mediterranean weather; but they go to Spain because their free hours aren't free.

For most, work and what comes with it have the eroding effect of chronic injury.

—

Technology is at its best when it is invisible.

—

The difference between true life and modern life equals the one between a conversation and bilateral recitations.

—

When I look at people on treadmills I wonder how alpha lions, the strongest, expend the least amount of energy, sleeping twenty hours a day; others hunt for them. *Caesar pontem fecit.**

—

Every social association that is not face-to-face is injurious to your health.

---

* Literally, "Caesar built a bridge," but the subtlety is that it can also suggest that "he had a bridge built for him."

THE REPUBLIC
OF LETTERS

Writing is the art of repeating oneself without anyone noticing.

Most people write so they can remember things; I write to forget.

What they call philosophy I call literature; what they call literature I call journalism; what they call journalism I call gossip; and what they call gossip I call (generously) voyeurism.

Writers are remembered for their best work, politicians for their worst mistakes, and businessmen are almost never remembered.

—

Critics may appear to blame the author for not writing the book they wanted to read; but in truth they are blaming him for writing the book they wanted, but were unable, to write.

—

Literature is not about promoting qualities, rather, airbrushing (your) defects.

—

For pleasure, read one chapter by Nabokov. For punishment, two.

—

There is a distinction between expressive hypochondria and literature, just as there is one between self-help and philosophy.

You need to keep reminding yourself of the obvious: charm lies in the unsaid, the unwritten, and the undisplayed. It takes mastery to control silence.

—

No author should be considered as having failed until he starts teaching others about writing.

—

Hard science gives sensational results with a horribly boring process; philosophy gives boring results with a sensational process; literature gives sensational results with a sensational process; and economics gives boring results with a boring process.

—

A good maxim allows you to have the last word without even starting a conversation.

Just as there are authors who enjoy having written and others who enjoy writing, there are books you enjoy reading and others you enjoy having read.

—

A genius is someone with flaws harder to imitate than his qualities.

—

With regular books, read the text and skip the footnotes; with those written by academics, read the footnotes and skip the text; and with business books, skip both the text and the footnotes.

—

Double a man's erudition; you will halve his citations.

Losers, when commenting on the works of someone patently more impressive, feel obligated to unnecessarily bring down their subject by expressing what he is not ("he is not a genius, but . . ."; "while he is no Leonardo . . .") instead of expressing what he is.

—

You are alive in inverse proportion to the density of clichés in your writing.

—

What we call "business books" is an eliminative category invented by bookstores for writings that have no depth, no style, no empirical rigor, and no linguistic sophistication.

—

Just like poets and artists, bureaucrats are born, not made; it takes normal humans extraordinary effort to keep attention on such boring tasks.

The costs of specialization: architects build to impress other architects; models are thin to impress other models; academics write to impress other academics; filmmakers try to impress other filmmakers; painters impress art dealers; but authors who write to impress book editors tend to fail.

—

It is a waste of emotions to answer critics; better to stay in print long after they are dead.

—

I can predict when an author is about to plagiarize me, and poorly so when he writes that Taleb "popularized" the theory of Black Swan events.*

—

Newspaper readers exposed to real prose are like deaf persons at a Puccini opera: they may like a thing or two while wondering, "what's the point?"

---

* It is also an indicator that he will imitate, "me, too" style, my business.

Some books cannot be summarized (real literature, poetry); some can be compressed to about ten pages; the majority to zero pages.

—

The exponential information age is like a verbally incontinent person: he talks more and more as fewer and fewer people listen.

—

What we call fiction is, when you look deep, much less fictional than nonfiction; but it is usually less imaginative.

—

It's much harder to write a book review for a book you've read than for a book you haven't read.

—

Most so-called writers keep writing and writing with the hope to, some day, find something to say.

Today, we mostly face the choice between those who write clearly about a subject they don't understand and those who write poorly about a subject they don't understand.

—

The information-rich Dark Ages: in 2010, 600,000 books were published, just in English, with few memorable quotes. Circa AD zero, a handful of books were written. In spite of the few that survived, there are loads of quotes.

—

In the past, most were ignorant, one in a thousand were refined enough to talk to. Today, literacy is higher, but thanks to progress, the media, and finance, only one in ten thousand.

—

We are better at (involuntarily) doing out of the box than (voluntarily) thinking out of the box.

Half of suckerhood is not realizing that what you don't like might be loved by someone else (hence by you, later), and the reverse.

—

It is much less dangerous to think like a man of action than to act like a man of thought.

—

Literature comes alive when covering up vices, defects, weaknesses, and confusions; it dies with every trace of preaching.

THE UNIVERSAL
AND
THE PARTICULAR

What I learned on my own I still remember.

—

Regular minds find similarities in stories (and situations); finer minds detect differences.

—

To grasp the difference between Universal and Particular, consider that some dress better to impress a single, specific person than an entire crowd.

We unwittingly amplify commonalities with friends, dissimilarities with strangers, and contrasts with enemies.

—

Many are so unoriginal they study history to find mistakes to repeat.

—

There is nothing deemed harmful (in general) that cannot be beneficial in some particular instances, and nothing deemed beneficial that cannot harm you in some circumstances. The more complex the system, the weaker the notion of Universal.

—

The fool generalizes the particular; the nerd particularizes the general; some do both; and the wise does neither.

You want to be yourself, idiosyncratic; the collective (school, rules, jobs, technology) wants you generic to the point of castration.

—

True love is the complete victory of the particular over the general, and the unconditional over the conditional.

FOOLED BY
RANDOMNESS

Unless we manipulate our surroundings, we have as little control over what and whom we think about as we do over the muscles of our hearts.

—

Corollary to Moore's Law: every ten years, collective wisdom degrades by half.*

* Moore's Law stipulates that computational power doubles every eighteen months.

Never rid anyone of an illusion unless you can replace it in his mind with another illusion. (But don't work too hard on it; the replacement illusion does not even have to be more convincing than the initial one.)

—

The tragedy is that much of what you think is random is in your control and, what's worse, the opposite.

—

The fool views himself as more unique and others more generic; the wise views himself as more generic and others more unique.

—

What made medicine fool people for so long was that its successes were prominently displayed and its mistakes (literally) buried.

—

The sucker's trap is when you focus on what you know and what others don't know, rather than the reverse.

Medieval man was a cog in a wheel he did not understand; modern man is a cog in a complicated system he thinks he understands.

—

The calamity of the information age is that the toxicity of data increases much faster than its benefits.

—

The role of the media is best seen in the journey from Cato the Elder to a modern politician.* Do some extrapolation if you want to be scared.

—

Mental clarity is the child of courage, not the other way around.†

---

* Say, Sarah Palin.
† The biggest error since Socrates has been to believe that lack of clarity is the source of all our ills, not the result of them.

Most info-Web-media-newspaper types have a hard time swallowing the idea that knowledge is reached (mostly) by removing junk from people's heads.

–

Finer men tolerate others' small inconsistencies though not the large ones; the weak tolerate others' large inconsistencies though not small ones.

–

Randomness is indistinguishable from complicated, undetected, and undetectable order; but order itself is indistinguishable from artful randomness.

AESTHETICS

Art is a one-sided conversation with the unobserved.

—

The genius of Benoît Mandelbrot is in achieving aesthetic simplicity without having recourse to smoothness.

—

Beauty is enhanced by unashamed irregularities; magnificence by a façade of blunder.

To understand "progress": all places we call ugly are both man-made and modern (Newark), never natural or historical (Rome).

—

We love imperfection, the right kind of imperfection; we pay up for original art and typo-laden first editions.

—

Most people need to wait for another person to say "this is beautiful art" to say "this is beautiful art"; some need to wait for two or more.

—

Almutanabbi boasted that he was the greatest of all Arab poets, but he said so in the greatest of all Arab poems.

—

Wit seduces by signaling intelligence without nerdiness.

In classical renderings of prominent figures, males are lean and females are plump; in modern photographs, the opposite.

—

Just as no monkey is as good-looking as the ugliest of humans, no academic is worthier than the worst of the creators.

—

If you want to annoy a poet, explain his poetry.

ETHICS

If you find any reason why you and someone are friends, you are not friends.

—

My biggest problem with modernity may lie in the growing separation of the ethical and the legal.*

---

* Former U.S. Treasury secretary "bankster" Robert Rubin, perhaps the biggest thief in history, broke no law. The difference between legal and ethical increases in a complex system . . . then blows it up.

Life's beauty: the kindest act toward you in your life may come from an outsider not interested in reciprocation.*

—

We are most motivated to help those who need us the least.

—

To value a person, consider the difference between how impressive he or she was at the first encounter and the most recent one.

—

Meditation is a way to be narcissistic without hurting anyone.

* The flip side: the worst pain inflicted on you will come from someone who at some point in your life cared about you.

True humility is when you can surprise yourself more than others; the rest is either shyness or good marketing.

—

We find it to be in extremely bad taste for individuals to boast of their accomplishments; but when countries do so we call it "national pride."

—

You can only convince people who think they can benefit from being convinced.

—

Greatness starts with the replacement of hatred with polite disdain.

—

Trust people who make a living lying down or standing up more than those who do so sitting down.

The tragedy of virtue is that the more obvious, boring, unoriginal, and sermonizing the proverb, the harder it is to implement.

—

Even the cheapest misers can be generous with advice.

—

If you lie to me, keep lying; don't hurt me by suddenly telling the truth.

—

Don't trust a man who needs an income—except if it is minimum wage.*

—

You may outlive your strength, never your wisdom.

* Those in corporate captivity would do anything to "feed a family."

Weak men act to satisfy their needs, stronger men their duties.

–

Religions and ethics have evolved from promising heaven if you do good, to promising heaven while you do good, to making you promise to do good.

–

Avoid calling heroes those who had no other choice.

–

There are those who will thank you for what you gave them and others who will blame you for what you did not give them.

–

Ethical man accords his profession to his beliefs, instead of according his beliefs to his profession. This has been rarer and rarer since the Middle Ages.

I trust everyone except those who tell me they are trustworthy.

—

People often need to suspend their self-promotion, and have someone in their lives they do not need to impress. This explains dog ownership.

—

Pure generosity is when you help the ingrate. Every other form is self-serving.*

—

I wonder if crooks can conceive that honest people can be shrewder than they.

—

In Proust there is a character, Morel, who demonizes Nissim Bernard, a Jew who lent him money, and becomes anti-Semitic just so he can escape the feeling of gratitude.

* Kantian ethics.

Promising someone good luck as a reward for good deeds sounds like a bribe—perhaps the remnant of an archaic, pre-deontic pre-classical morality.

—

The difference between magnificence and arrogance is in what one does when nobody is looking.

—

The nation-state: apartheid without political incorrectness.

—

In a crowd of a hundred, 50 percent of the wealth, 90 percent of the imagination, and 100 percent of the intellectual courage will reside in a single person—not necessarily the same one.

—

Just as dyed hair makes older men less attractive, it is what you do to hide your weaknesses that makes them repugnant.

For soldiers, we use the term "mercenary," but we absolve employees of responsibility with "everybody needs to make a living."

—

English does not distinguish between arrogant-up (irreverence toward the temporarily powerful) and arrogant-down (directed at the small guy).

—

Someone from your social class who becomes poor affects you more than thousands of starving ones outside of it.

ROBUSTNESS
AND
FRAGILITY

You are only secure if you can lose your fortune without the additional worse insult of having to become humble.*

—

To test someone's robustness to reputational errors, ask a man in front of an audience if he is "still doing poorly" or if he is "still losing money" and watch his reaction.

* My great-great-great-great-great grandfather's rule.

Robustness is progress without impatience.

—

When conflicted between two choices, take neither.

—

Nation-states like war; city-states like commerce; families like stability; and individuals like entertainment.

—

Robust is when you care more about the few who like your work than the multitude who dislike it (artists); fragile when you care more about the few who dislike your work than the multitude who like it (politicians).

—

The rationalist imagines an imbecile-free society; the empiricist an imbecile-proof one, or, even better, a rationalist-proof one.

Academics are only useful when they try to be useless (say, as in mathematics and philosophy) and dangerous when they try to be useful.

—

For the robust, an error is information; for the fragile, an error is an error.

—

The best test of robustness to reputational damage is your emotional state (fear, joy, boredom) when you get an email from a journalist.

—

The main disadvantage of being a writer, particularly in Britain, is that there is nothing you can do in public or private that would damage your reputation.

Passionate hate (by nations and individuals) ends by rotation to another subject of hate; mediocrity cannot handle more than one enemy. This makes warring statelings with shifting alliances and enmities a robust system.

—

I find it inconsistent (and corrupt) to dislike big government while favoring big business—but (alas) not the reverse.

—

How often have you arrived one, three, or six hours late on a transatlantic flight as opposed to one, three, or six hours early? This explains why deficits tend to be larger, rarely smaller, than planned.

THE LUDIC
FALLACY AND
DOMAIN
DEPENDENCE*

Sports are commoditized and, alas, prostituted randomness.

—

When you beat up someone physically, you get exercise and stress relief; when you assault him verbally on the Internet, you just harm yourself.

* *Ludic* is Latin for "related to games"; the fallacy prevalent in *The Black Swan* about making life resemble games (or formal setups) with crisp rules rather than the reverse. Domain dependence is when one acts in a certain way in an environment (say, the gym) and a different way in another.

Just as smooth surfaces, competitive sports, and specialized work fossilize mind and body, competitive academia fossilizes the soul.

—

They agree that chess training only improves chess skills but disagree that classroom training (almost) only improves classroom skills.

—

Upon arriving at the hotel in Dubai, the businessman had a porter carry his luggage; I later saw him lifting free weights in the gym.

—

Games were created to give nonheroes the illusion of winning. In real life, you don't know who really won or lost (except too late), but you can tell who is heroic and who is not.

I suspect that IQ, SAT, and school grades are tests designed by nerds so they can get high scores in order to call each other intelligent.*

—

They read Gibbon's *Decline and Fall* on an eReader but refuse to drink Château Lynch-Bages in a Styrofoam cup.

—

My best example of the domain dependence of our minds, from my recent visit to Paris: at lunch in a French restaurant, my friends ate the salmon and threw away the skin; at dinner, at a sushi bar, the very same friends ate the skin and threw away the salmon.

—

Fragility: we have been progressively separating human courage from warfare, allowing wimps with computer skills to kill people without the slightest risk to their lives.

* Smart and wise people who score low on IQ tests, or patently intellectually defective ones, like former U.S. president George W. Bush, who score high on them (130), are testing the test and not the reverse.

EPISTEMOLOGY
AND SUBTRACTIVE
KNOWLEDGE

Since Plato, Western thought and the theory of knowledge have focused on the notions of True-False; as commendable as it was, it is high time to shift the concern to Robust-Fragile, and social epistemology to the more serious problem of Sucker-Nonsucker.

—

The problem of knowledge is that there are many more books on birds written by ornithologists than books on birds written by birds and books on ornithologists written by birds.

The perfect sucker understands that pigs can stare at pearls but doesn't realize he can be in an analog situation.

—

It takes extraordinary wisdom and self-control to accept that many things have a logic we do not understand that is smarter than our own.

—

Knowledge is subtractive, not additive—what we subtract (reduction by what does not work, what *not* to do), not what we add (what to do).*

—

They think that intelligence is about noticing things that are relevant (detecting patterns); in a complex world, intelligence consists in ignoring things that are irrelevant (avoiding false patterns).

* The best way to spot a charlatan: someone (like a consultant or a stockbroker) who tells you what to do instead of what *not* to do.

Happiness; we don't know what it means, how to measure it, or how to reach it, but we know extremely well how to avoid unhappiness.

—

The imagination of the genius vastly surpasses his intellect; the intellect of the academic vastly surpasses his imagination.

—

The ideal *trivium* education, and the least harmful one to society and pupils, would be mathematics, logic, and Latin; a double dose of Latin authors to compensate for the severe loss of wisdom that comes from mathematics; just enough mathematics and logic to control verbiage and rhetoric.

—

The four most influential moderns: Darwin, Marx, Freud, and (the productive) Einstein were scholars but not academics. It has always been hard to do genuine—and nonperishable—work within institutions.

THE SCANDAL OF
PREDICTION

A prophet is not someone with special visions, just
someone blind to most of what others see.

—

For the ancients, forecasting historical events was an
insult to the God(s); for me, it is an insult to man—
that is, for some, to science.

—

The ancients knew very well that the only way to
understand events was to cause them.

Anyone voicing a forecast or expressing an opinion without something at risk has some element of phoniness. Unless he risks going down with the ship this would be like watching an adventure movie.

—

They would take forecasting more seriously if it were pointed out to them that in Semitic languages the words for forecast and "prophecy" are the same.

—

For Seneca, the Stoic sage should withdraw from public efforts when unheeded and the state is corrupt beyond repair. It is wiser to wait for self-destruction.

BEING A
PHILOSOPHER
AND MANAGING
TO REMAIN ONE

To become a philosopher, start by walking very slowly.

—

Real mathematicians understand completeness, real philosophers understand incompleteness, the rest don't formally understand anything.

—

In twenty-five centuries, no human came along with the brilliance, depth, elegance, wit, and imagination to match Plato—to protect us from his legacy.

Why do I have an obsessive Plato problem? Most people need to surpass their predecessors; Plato managed to surpass all his successors.

—

To be a philosopher is to know through long walks, by reasoning, and reasoning only, *a priori*, what others can only potentially learn from their mistakes, crises, accidents, and bankruptcies—that is, *a posteriori*.

—

Engineers can compute but not define, mathematicians can define but not compute, economists can neither define nor compute.

—

Something finite but with unknown upper bounds is epistemically equivalent to something infinite. This is epistemic infinity.

Conscious ignorance, if you can practice it, expands your world; it can make things infinite.

—

For the classics, philosophical insight was the product of a life of leisure; for me, a life of leisure is the product of philosophical insight.

—

It takes a lot of intellect and confidence to accept that what makes sense doesn't really make sense.

—

A theological Procrustean bed: for the Orthodox since Gregory Palamas and for the Arabs since Algazel, attempts to define God using the language of philosophical universals were a rationalistic mistake. I am still waiting for a modern to take notice.

Saying "the mathematics of uncertainty" is like saying "the chastity of sex"—what is mathematized is no longer uncertain, and vice versa.

—

Sadly, we learn the most from fools, economists, and other reverse role models, yet we pay them back with the worst ingratitude.

—

In Plato's *Protagoras,* Socrates contrasts philosophy as the collaborative search for truth with the sophist's use of rhetoric to gain the upper hand in argument for fame and money. Twenty-five centuries later, this is exactly the salaried researcher and the modern tenure-loving academic. Progress.

ECONOMIC LIFE
AND OTHER VERY
VULGAR SUBJECTS

There are designations, like "economist," "prostitute,"
or "consultant," for which additional characterization
doesn't add information.

—

A mathematician starts with a problem and creates a
solution; a consultant starts by offering a "solution"
and creates a problem.

—

What they call "risk" I call opportunity; but what they
call "low risk" opportunity I call sucker problem.

Organizations are like caffeinated dupes unknowingly jogging backward; you only hear of the few who reach their destination.

—

The best test of whether someone is extremely stupid (or extremely wise) is whether financial and political news makes sense to him.

—

The left holds that because markets are stupid models should be smart; the right believes that because models are stupid markets should be smart. Alas, it never hit both sides that both markets and models are very stupid.

—

Economics is like a dead star that still seems to produce light; but you know it is dead.

Suckers think that you cure greed with money, addiction with substances, expert problems with experts, banking with bankers, economics with economists, and debt crises with debt spending.

—

You can be certain that the head of a corporation has a lot to worry about when he announces publicly that "there is nothing to worry about."

—

The stock market, in brief: participants are calmly waiting in line to be slaughtered while thinking it is for a Broadway show.

—

The main difference between government bailouts and smoking is that in some rare cases the statement "this is my last cigarette" holds true.

What makes us fragile is that institutions cannot have the same virtues (honor, truthfulness, courage, loyalty, tenacity) as individuals.

—

The worst damage has been caused by competent people trying to do good; the best improvements have been brought by incompetent ones *not* trying to do good.

—

The difference between banks and the Mafia: banks have better legal-regulatory expertise, but the Mafia understands public opinion.

—

"It is much easier to scam people for billions than for just millions."*

---

* Inspired by the Madoff episode.

At a panel in Moscow, I watched the economist Edmund Phelps, who got the "Nobel" for writings no one reads, theories no one uses, and lectures no one understands.

—

One of the failures of "scientific approximation" in the nonlinear domain comes from the inconvenient fact that the average of expectations is different from the expectation of averages.*

—

Journalists as reverse aphorists: my statement "you need skills to get a BMW, skills plus luck to become a Warren Buffett" was summarized as "Taleb says Buffett has *no* skills."

—

The curious mind embraces science; the gifted and sensitive, the arts; the practical, business; the leftover becomes an economist.

---

* Don't cross a river, because it is on average four feet deep. This is also known as Jensen's inequality.

Public companies, like human cells, are programmed for apoptosis, suicide through debt and hidden risks. Bailouts invest the process with a historical dimension.

—

In poor countries, officials receive explicit bribes; in D.C. they get the sophisticated implicit, unspoken promise to work for large corporations.

—

Fate is at its cruelest when a banker ends up in poverty.

—

We should make students recompute their GPAs by counting their grades in finance and economics backward.

—

The agency problem drives every company, thanks to the buildup of hidden risks, to maximal fragility.

In politics we face the choice between warmongering, nation-state-loving, big-business agents on one hand; and risk-blind, top-down, epistemic arrogant big servants of large employers on the other. But we have a choice.

THE SAGE,
THE WEAK,
AND
THE MAGNIFICENT*

Mediocre men tend to be outraged by small insults but passive, subdued, and silent in front of very large ones.†

—

The only definition of an alpha male: if you try to be an alpha male, you will never be one.

* In Aristotle's *Nicomachean Ethics,* the megalopsychos, which I translate as the magnificent, is the "great-souled" who thinks of himself as worthy of great things and, aware of his own position in life, abides by a certain system of ethics that excludes pettiness. This notion of great soul, though displaced by Christian ethics advocating humility, remains present in Levantine culture, with the literal *Kabir al-nafs.* Among other attributes, the magnificent walks slowly.
† Consider the reaction to the banking and economics establishments.

Those who have nothing to prove never say that they have nothing to prove.

—

The weak shows his strength and hides his weaknesses; the magnificent exhibits his weaknesses like ornaments.

—

How superb to become wise without being boring; how sad to be boring without being wise.*

—

The traits I respect are erudition and the courage to stand up when half-men are afraid for their reputation. Any idiot can be intelligent.

—

The mediocre regret their words more than their silence; finer men regret their silence more than their words; the magnificent has nothing to regret.

* Looking at Federal Reserve Chairman Ben Bernanke.

Regular men are a certain varying number of meals away from lying, stealing, killing, or even working as forecasters for the Federal Reserve in Washington; never the magnificent.*

—

Social science means inventing a certain brand of human we can understand.

—

When expressing "good luck" to a peer, the weak wishes the opposite; the strong is mildly indifferent; but only the magnificent means it.

—

In the past, only some of the males, but all of the females, were able to procreate. Equality is more natural for females.

---

* I had to read Aristotle's *Nicomachean Ethics* Book IV ten times before realizing what he didn't say explicitly (but knew): the magnificent (megalopsychos) is all about unconditionals.

The magnificent believes half of what he hears and twice what he says.

—

A verbal threat is the most authentic certificate of impotence.

—

The two most celebrated acts of courage in history aren't Homeric fighters but two Eastern Mediterranean fellows who died, even sought death, for their ideas.

—

The weak cannot be good; or, perhaps, he can only be good within an exhaustive and overreaching legal system.

—

By all means, avoid words—threats, complaints, justification, narratives, reframing, attempts to win arguments, supplications; avoid words!

According to Lucian of Samosata, the philosopher Demonax stopped a Spartan from beating his servant. "You are making him your equal," he said.

—

The classical man's worst fear was inglorious death; the modern man's worst fear is just death.

THE IMPLICIT AND
THE EXPLICIT

You know you have influence when people start noticing your absence more than the presence of others.

—

You are guaranteed a repetition when you hear the declaration "never again!"

—

Some reticent people use silence to conceal their intelligence; but most do so to hide the lack of it.

When someone says "I am not that stupid," it often means that he is more stupid than he thinks.

—

Bad-mouthing is the only genuine, never faked expression of admiration.

—

When a woman says about a man that he is intelligent, she often means handsome; when a man says about a woman that she is dumb, he always means attractive.

—

What organized dating sites fail to understand is that people are far more interesting in what they don't say about themselves.

—

For company, you often prefer those who find *you* interesting over those you find interesting.

—

The Internet broke the private-public wall; impulsive and inelegant utterances that used to be kept private are now available for literal interpretation.

One of the problems with social networks is that it is getting harder and harder for others to complain about you behind your back.

—

You can be certain that a person has the means but not the will to help you when he says "there is nothing else I can do." And you can be certain that a person has neither means nor will to help you when he says "I am here to help."

—

We expect places and products to be less attractive than in marketing brochures, but we never forgive humans for being worse than their first impressions.

—

When someone starts a sentence with "simply," you should expect to hear something very complicated.

—

Half the people lie with their lips; the other half with their tears.

ON THE VARIETIES OF LOVE AND NONLOVE

At any stage, humans can thirst for money, knowledge, or love; sometimes for two, never for three.

—

Love without sacrifice is like theft.

—

Marriage is the institutional process of feminizing men—and feminizing women.

There are men who surround themselves with women (and seek wealth) for ostentation; others who do so mostly for consumption; they are rarely the same.

—

Outside of friendship and love, it is very hard to find situations with bilateral, two-way suckers.

—

I attended a symposium, an event named after a fifth-century (B.C.) Athenian drinking party in which nonnerds talked about love; alas, there was no drinking and, mercifully, nobody talked about love.

—

You will get the most attention from those who hate you. No friend, no admirer, and no partner will flatter you with as much curiosity.

When a young woman partners with an otherwise uninteresting rich man, she can sincerely believe that she is attracted to some very specific body part (say, his nose, neck, or knee).

—

A good foe is far more loyal, far more predictable, and, to the clever, far more useful than the most valuable admirer.

—

If my detractors knew me better they would hate me even more.

THE END

Platonic minds expect life to be like film, with defined terminal endings; a-Platonic ones expect film to be like life and, except for a few irreversible conditions such as death, distrust the terminal nature of all human-declared endings.

POSTFACE

The general theme of my work is the limitations of human knowledge, and the charming and less charming errors and biases when working with matters that lie outside our field of observation, the unobserved and the unobservables—the unknown; what lies on the other side of the veil of opacity.

Because our minds need to reduce information, we are more likely to try to squeeze a phenomenon into the Procrustean bed of a crisp and known category (amputating the unknown), rather than suspend categorization, and make it tangible. Thanks to our detections of false patterns, along with real ones, what is random will appear less random and more certain—our overactive brains are more likely to impose the wrong, simplistic narrative than no narrative at all.*

The mind can be a wonderful tool for self-delusion—it

---

* This discounting of the unseen comes from the human "scorn of the abstract" (our minds are not good at handling the non-anecdotal and tend to be swayed by vivid imagery, making the media distort our view of the world).

was not designed to deal with complexity and nonlinear uncertainties.* Counter to the common discourse, *more information means more delusions:* our detection of false patterns is growing faster and faster as a side effect of modernity and the information age: there is this mismatch between the messy randomness of the information-rich current world, with its complex interactions, and our intuitions of events, derived in a simpler ancestral habitat. Our mental architecture is at an increased mismatch with the world in which we live.

This leads to sucker problems: when the map does not correspond to the territory, there is a certain category of fool—the overeducated, the academic, the journalist, the newspaper reader, the mechanistic "scientist," the pseudo-empiricist, those endowed with what I call "epistemic arrogance," this wonderful ability to discount what they did not see, the unobserved—who enter a state of denial, imagining the territory as fitting his map. More generally, the fool here is someone who does the wrong reduction for the sake of reduction, or removes something essential, cutting off the legs, or, better, part of the head of a visitor while insisting that he preserved his persona with 95 percent accuracy. Look around at the Procrustean beds we've

---

* Nor is science capable of dealing effectively with nonlinear and complex matters, those fraught with interdependence (climate, economic life, the human body), in spite of its hyped-up successes in the linear domain (physics and engineering), which give it a prestige that has endangered us.

created, some beneficial, some more questionable: regulations, top-down governments, academia, gyms, commutes, high-rise office buildings, involuntary human relationships, employment, etc.

Since the Enlightenment, in the great tension between *rationalism* (how we would like things to be so they make sense to us) and *empiricism* (how things are), we have been blaming the world for not fitting the beds of "rational" models, have tried to change humans to fit technology, fudged our ethics to fit our needs for employment, asked economic life to fit the theories of economists, and asked human life to squeeze into some narrative.

We are robust when errors in the representation of the unknown and understanding of random effects do not lead to adverse outcomes—fragile otherwise. The robust benefits from Black Swan events,* the fragile is severely hit by them. We are more and more fragile to a certain brand of scientific autism making confident claims about the unknown—leading to expert problems, risk, massive dependence on human error. As the reader can see from my aphorisms, I have respect for mother nature's methods of robustness (billions of years allow most of what is fragile to break); classical thought is more robust (in its re-

---

* A Black Swan (capitalized) is an event (historical, economic, technological, personal) that is both unpredicted by some observer and carries massive consequences. In spite of growth in our knowledge, the role of these Black Swans has been growing.

spect for the unknown, the epistemic humility) than the modern post-Enlightenment naïve pseudoscientific autism. Thus my classical values make me advocate the triplet of erudition, elegance, and courage; against modernity's phoniness, nerdiness, and philistinism.*

Art is robust; science, not always (to put it mildly). Some Procrustean beds make life worth living: art and, the most potent of all, the poetic aphorism.

Aphorisms, maxims, proverbs, short sayings, even, to some extent, epigrams are the earliest literary form—often integrated into what we now call poetry. They carry the cognitive compactness of the sound bite (though both more potent and more elegant than today's down-market version),† with some show of bravado in the ability of the author to compress powerful ideas in a handful of words—particularly in an oral format. Indeed, it had to be bravado, because the Arabic word for an improvised one-liner is "act of manliness," though such a notion of "manliness" is

---

* Many philistines reduce my ideas to an opposition to technology when in fact I am opposing the naïve blindness to its side effects—the fragility criterion. I'd rather be unconditional about ethics and conditional about technology than the reverse.

† Note the distinction from TV one-liners: the sound bite loses information; the aphorism gains. Somehow, aphorisms obey the Gigerenzer and Goldstein "less is more" effect.

less gender-driven than it sounds and can be equally translated as "the skills of being human" (*virtue* has the same roots in Latin, *vir,* "man"). As if those who could produce powerful thoughts in such a way were invested with talismanic powers.

This mode is at the center of the Levantine soul (and the broader Eastern Mediterranean). When God spoke to the Semites, he spoke in very short poetic sentences, usually through the mouths of prophets. Consider the Scriptures, more particularly the books of Proverbs and Ecclesiastes; Islam's holy book, the Koran, is a collection of concentrated aphorisms. And the format has been adopted for synthetic literary prophecies: Nietzsche's *Zarathustra,* or, more recently, my compatriot from a neighboring (and warring) village in northern Lebanon, Kahlil Gibran, author of *The Prophet.*

Outside of what we now call religion, take the aphorisms of Heraclitus and Hippocrates; the works of Publilius Syrus (a Syrian slave who owed his freedom to his eloquence, expressed in his *Sententiae,* potent one-line poems that echo in the maxims of La Rochefoucauld), and the poetry of the poet who is broadly considered the greatest of all Arab poets, Almutanabbi.

Aphorisms as stand-alone sentences have been used for exposition, for religious text, for advice to a grandchild by a Levantine grandmother, for boasting (as I said earlier, in an aphorism, Almutanabbi used them to tell us, convincingly, that he was the greatest Arab poet), for satires* (Martial, Aesop, Almaarri), by the *moralistes* (Vaugenargues, La Rochefoucauld, La Bruyère, Chamfort), to expose opaque philosophy (Wittgenstein), relatively clearer ones (Schopenhauer, Nietzsche, Cioran), or crystal-clear ideas (Pascal).† You never have to explain an aphorism—like poetry, this is something that the reader needs to deal with by himself.‡

There are bland aphorisms, the platitudinous ones harboring important truths that you had thought about before (the kind that make intelligent people recoil at Gibran's *The Prophet*); pleasant ones, those you never thought about but trigger in you the *Aha!* of an important discovery (such as those in La Rochefoucauld); but the best are those you did not think about before, and for which it takes you more than one reading to realize that

---

* The best way to measure the loss of intellectual sophistication in the Internet age—this "nerdification," to put it bluntly—is in the growing disappearance of sarcasm, as mechanistic minds take insults a bit too literally.
† It is not uncommon to find the same maxim repeated by several authors separated by a millennium or a continent.
‡ The aphorism has been somewhat debased (outside the German language) by its association with witticism, such as the ones by Oscar Wilde, Mark Twain, Ambrose Bierce, or Sacha Guitry—deep thought can be poetic and witty, as with Schopenhauer, Nietzsche, or (sometimes) Wittgenstein; but, abiding by the distinction between Sacred and Profane, philosophy and poetry are not stand-up comedy.

they are important truths, particularly when the silent character of the truth in them is so powerful that they are forgotten as soon as read.

Aphorisms require us to change our reading habits and approach them in small doses; each one of them is a complete unit, a complete narrative dissociated from others.

My best definition of a nerd: someone who asks you to explain an aphorism.

I have been aware that my style was aphoristic. As a teenager, I was mentored by the poet Georges Schéhadé (his poetry reads like proverbs), who predicted that I would see the light and grow up to make a career in poetry, once I got this ideas business out of my system. More recently, readers have triggered numerous copyright alerts by posting quotes from my books on the Web, but I had never thought of re-expressing my ideas (or, rather, my central idea about the limits of knowledge) in such a way until I realized that these sentences come naturally to me, almost involuntarily, in an eerie way, particularly when walking (slowly) or when freeing up my mind to do nothing, or nothing effortful—I could convince myself that I was hearing voices from the other side of the veil of opacity.

By setting oneself totally free of constraints, free of thoughts, free of this debilitating activity called work, free of efforts, elements hidden in the texture of reality start staring at you; then mysteries that you never thought existed emerge in front of your eyes.

ACKNOWLEDGMENTS

P. Tanous, L. de Chantal, B. Oppetit, M. Blyth, N. Vardy, B. Appleyard, C. Mihailescu, J. Baz, B. Dupire, Y. Zilber, S. Roberts, A. Pilpel, W. Goodlad, W. Murphy, M. Brockman, J. Brockman, C. Taleb, C. Sandis, J. Kujat, T. Burnham, R. Dobelli, M. Ghosn (the younger), S. Taleb, D. Riviere, J. Gray, M. Carreira, M.-C. Riachi, P. Bevelin, J. Audi (*pontem fecit*), S. Roberts, B. Flyvberg, E. Boujaoude, P. Boghossian, S. Riley, G. Origgi, S. Ammons, and many more (I sometimes remember names of critically helpful people when it is too late to show gratitude).

ABOUT THE AUTHOR

NASSIM NICHOLAS TALEB spends most of his time as a flâneur, meditating in cafés across the planet. A former trader, he is currently Distinguished Professor at New York University. He is the author of *Fooled by Randomness* and *The Black Swan*, which has spent more than a year on the *New York Times* bestseller list and has become an intellectual, social, and cultural touchstone.